KT-468-039

Acknowledgements

To some of the people who have shared a big part of this life with me.

Joe Pyle Snr – Ted Pyle – Jean Pyle – Lorraine Pyle – Den Phinbow – Alex Steene – Charlie Richardson – Ronnie Kray – Charlie Kray – Peter Brayham Wilf Pine – Bruce Reynolds – Mitch – Alan – Teddy – Alan Paramasivan – Rod Doll – Mike Biggs – Ronnie Biggs – Steve Slater – Paul Ferris – Steven Wraith – Christian Simpson – Rob Davis – Richard Hunt Snr & Jnr – Eddie Cox – Johnny Edwards – Lewis Edwards – Ricky English – Cream – Marc Carey – Dave Courtney – Brendan McGir – Welsh Phill Davies – Sven Hamer – Gary Sayer – Fred Batt – Brian Harvey – Rob Davis – Baz Allen Johhny Corbett – Richard Mallett – Andy Hollinson – Warren – Alan D – Ade – Johnny Crittenden- Ori Spado – Anthony Spado – Tommy Saulo – Greg Steene – Harry Holland – Tony Lambrianou – John Nash – Jim Nash – Roy Nash – Ronnie Nash – The RoseHill lads – Shawn B – Lady Janet Neaves – Gary C London – and to all of those I can't name because you would get me in bloody trouble x

JOEY PYLE JNR

From **VILLIAN**
To
VERSE-MAKER

First published in 2017 by:
Britain's Next Bestseller
An imprint of Live It Publishing
27 Old Gloucester Road
London.
United Kingdom
WC1N 3AX

All enquiries should be addressed to info@bnbsbooks.co.uk

Cover design by Joseph Pyle Jnr

ISBN-13: 978-1-910565-97-1 (pbk)
Mobi: 978-1-910565-98-8
www.bnbsbooks.co.uk
@BNBSbooks

To Mum & Dad
I know you always did your best.

Suzanne and all my children and the newest member of
our family, Little Nate Joseph
and also some of the people I have had in my life and lost.
Joseph Henry Pyle, Catherine & Arthur (Arnie) Pyle,
my dear sister Sue, Uncle Den, Alec Steene, Roy Shaw,
Ronnie Kray, Charlie Richardson, Charlie Kray, Peter Tilly,
Terry Marshe, Johnny Nash, Danny Simms.

I MAY be in the world of business and a father now, but there was once a time when I led a very different life, a life that, believe me, you do not want to see. I was cold, calculated, almost inhuman and sat on the top table for many years. Be very careful where you tread because that side of me is not lost, I just choose not to use it anymore.

* * *

Is there such a wretched thing as betrayal?

Can one imagine anything more horrifying than those who once you called brother?

Conspire to bring forth your demise

Is there such a thing so cruel?

* * *

The greatest endowment God bestowed on man was the art of reason, then he took it away with emotion!

* * *

Only a man with sorrow in his heart can show mercy.

* * *

Reality... what is reality?

Only when you have wiped the blood from your hands can you realise what your life is worth.

'It's a Dog eat Dog world, always has been, and sadly... always will be... BUT THAT DOESN'T MEAN YOU HAVE TO BE A FUCKING DOG!'

Mitch Pyle, Warren, Joe Pyle Jr, Alan Pyle, Teddy Bam Bam

Photo credit: Jocelyn Bain Hogg

CRIME – criminal or gangster? Those are funny words which, to me, don't have much meaning. What is a fucking criminal? You read books about Al Capone who shot everyone in some far-off world called Chicago. But this is London, so people link the Krays to those words.

Straight-goers use words like these when they look down their noses and label you. The Krays weren't criminals to me, they were just three brothers who wanted to get ahead in life and made use of their talents. So, they killed someone. What's new... half of our so-called heroes have killed people.

Murder! That's another one of those words. If I kill someone, let's say just one person, then I'm a murderer. If I join the army and kill a hundred people, then I'm a soldier! What is the bigger crime? To kill one man, a man who might want to kill me or to kill a 100 nameless men because it's my job! Soldiers even get a priest or holy man giving them prayers before they go into battle.

The underworld is another word which some people like to label us, so if we are the underworld then who the fuck is the overworld. Everything has an opposite so where is the underworld's opposite?

If you weigh this up then you soon discover that the world we live in is not a fair world, the odds are stacked against you. It's a world of hypocrisy and double standards, where the real criminals dont' come from the poor parts of town.

Every so-called crime has a reason behind it. Some people murder because they are sick, some because they enjoy it, some do it for survival while others do it because there's no other choice. In these pages you will find some of the things you read very cold and to the point, but mostly you will read what it is like to live in a world few can judge.

If you are one of those people who likes to stick labels on people, then throw the fucking book in the bin! It's not for you! But if you have a heart and a soul then hopefully you'll understand the meanings behind the verses.

I think for the sake of this book, I'll go back to the top of the page and call the dark mysterious world I inhabit the underworld. Which then lends itself to a question – what is the underworld?

To me it's where I live. My domain, my life and the place where I feel most at home. From the day I was born I was introduced to what is known as the 'top table' of British crime.

Some say I'm a crook. Some say I am their father, others their pal and some that I have saved their lives. Whatever I am, I live life the way I want to live, always have done and always will.

Am I good or bad... I guess you'll just have to decide for yourselves?

* * *

Foreword

THAT smile, that glint, that sparkle in his eyes. Joey was only a little boy when I was introduced to him by his father and my friend, Joey Pyle. A little boy with sticky-out ears and a smile... that smile. He can break your heart with a look and then stitch it back up again in a moment with just a smile. He had an old head on very young shoulders and he carried it well. Surrounded by big, powerful men, Joey seemed at home. For me, these men and his Mum, Shirley, were the foundation of the man Joey has become.

A Good Man – A Good Fellow

Your friend
RAYMOND WINSTONE, from across the River

CLIVE BLACK (Best pal & Godfather to my son, Manny Pyle) MD of Blacklist Records Inc.:

When Joe asked me to write a foreword for his book of poetry I thought 'why me and what can I say'?

You see, when it comes to Joe and his world I never 'say' anything... it's better that way! _

I do often whisper to Joe my thoughts on life and try to give him advice from an angle others close to him may not dare to – you see what Joe is to me is just 'honest'. He says it as he sees it and holds zero back.

He is 'loyal' beyond the call of duty and over the last 20 years he has been my closest friend. The one I can rely on – no questions asked.

Charismatic and unreadable, Joe is a man of many layers... peel back the tough exterior of the gangster and you get the family man, the friend. Then there's the creative side. He writes, acts and dreams of making big things happen... he is a man of great depth and many dimensions.

His heart is so big that he spends all his profits making sure those around him are 'sweet'. Even the local hospitals and kids charities get 'looked after' anywhere Joe puts on an event. Looking after the locals is in his DNA. He comes from a stock where your turf was everything and the people who lived there needed to be looked after. Joe Snr was a massive figure in my life – full of wisdom. He said in a sentence what most took an hour to say, but the best thing about getting to know Joe Snr was one day he said to me 'meet my son you will get on great' and we really did and always will do – Joe and I are friends for life thanks to Joe Snr.

You feel safer in this mad world just knowing that Joe Pyle is your mate and on your side.

Now Joe – I hope you got some good rhymes in this book of yours and for Christ sake use spellcheck!

God Bless
Clive

JIMMY WHITE MBE (The people's champion & very good friend):

When Joe asked if I would do a foreword for his book of poetry, I didn't hesitate to say yes. I have known his father, Joe Snr, all of my life. Being a South London Tooting boy which was his father's stomping ground, we became good friends and from that friendship I got to know Joe Jnr who is around my age. We have had some blinding nights out together and share some very good friends. I wish him all the best with this book and hope everyone enjoys it. God bless and good luck with the book Joe, your Pal Jimmy White MBE

ORI SPADO (My Dad in Los Angeles)
Beverly Hills, California:

I first met young Joey when he was a young man and instantly I saw what his character was. I have watched him grow into a man. Not just kind to his friends and family, but he is there for them. But most important is his intellect of analysing a situation, getting the facts and then making his decision. If I were to write everything good, I could write another book. Those who know him then I must say hold your head high and be proud as there are few real men left and Joey is certainly one of them. In the years since his father and my dear mate passed, Joey has become my third son and I am proud of that. Although there is a big pond between us I wake every morning knowing if I needed him he would be here for me and me for him. In a fast changing world I can say from my heart I know this with confidence and as I learned in my life the only ones I can count on like that is my family and Joe is my family. LL&R Look in the dictionary and you will see Joey's name. I love you Joey.

FREDDIE FOREMAN:

I have known young Joe all his life. His book will be a big success of that I am sure. His dad would have been very proud.

WILF PINE (family friend and author of *Englishman and the Mafia*):

What can I say about this highly respected family? I have known 'Junior' as I call him all his life, he was a cheeky little sod and has been a lot of other things in his young life but he has always been loyal to his family ways and his family friends. His father was my dearest pal, the Boss of Bosses who even after we lost him ten years ago, I think of him every day. Junior is like his father, a man of honour and truth and someone you can rely on when you need to rely on someone. He is my best pal's son but I have no hesitation in calling him one of closest pals. Good luck with the book Junior, I know just like everything else you put that mind to, you will make a success of it. And kiss those lovely kids for me. *God Bless* Wilf.

MARK MORRISON (Return of the Mack):

To my brother Joe Jnr, my old manager and most trusted friend, Never stop being you, Joe. Brothers till the end of time; Mark (Peace)

SHIRLEY HINE (Mum):

My son Joey, I've known him for fifty years. I should do I'm his Mum! Good Luck with the book Joey. I'm sure you will be doing more, this is just the start of something new Your life is in the boxing. Nobody knows the time and effort you put in to it. You are so caring and you wear your heart on your sleeve. A family man and a true gent … knock you down and you will always get back up and try harder in whatever you do. Good luck Joey and get that film out there, my Joey.

MITCH PYLE (My Brother):

What can I say about this man that has not already been said? Except I have been a part of this family for 20 years now and was taken in by Joe Pyle sn. And the best thing to come of out this life is a man I can call my brother Joe Pyle jr. a man of Respect. A man with honour. A business man in many things. A man who stands by he's family no matter what it is. A man I call my brother. I love you and will always be by your side. Love loyalty & respect.

ALAN PYLE (My Brother):

Good luck with the book, Joe. You're my older brother and have always been there for me, no matter what the cost. I know you are always trying to look out for me and as brothers we are always there for each other, no matter what comes our way. Love ya. Al (HMP Wormwood Scrubs)

DAVE COURTNEY (Uncle Dave):

Hello people.

Firstly, may I say what an honour it is for me to have the privilege of writing a forward for a book that ain't a gangster orientated piece of literature. And for it to be for someone that happens to be more than a very, very good friend of mine is just excellent for me.

I have read through this book a number of times now and I must say that the more I read it the more I learn. I feel it is a real piece of wisdom from someone's mind that knew what he was talking about, and it shows in its truthfulness and honesty.

Sir Joey Pyle Snr, my mentor, also wrote a book of poetry whilst in prison and would have been very proud of his son's first publication which is also a book of poetry.

It's well worth a read and if you are intelligent enough to appreciate the knowledge and heartfelt emotions from someone's mind that knew what they were talking about, you would call it a classic.

So I am asking you, not telling you, just take my word for it that this book is the fucking bollox.com.

Dave Courtney OBE

VERONICA RICHARDSON (Wife to Charlie Richardson):

Charlie first introduced me to Joey's mum and Dad over 25 years ago. Little did I know then that they and Joe Jnr would become lifelong friends. Joe was a cheeky rascal then and we have watched him grow into a very handsome successful man. I know his Dad and my Charlie would be proud of today. I am honoured to be part of his and his beautiful families' life and I know he will only go upwards. Good luck with the book Joe xxx big hugs xx

STEVE WRAITH (The Geordie Connection! A man of many talents who is very dear to my heart):

Joe Pyle has been a good friend of mine for over 25 years now. We may live 350 miles apart but we are only ever a phone call away from each other. This man puts his life and soul into everything he does and is well respected the length and breadth of the UK. His talent knows no boundaries as this book shows. Good luck brother...

ANTHONY SPADO (Brother from the USA)

OCS Entertainment, Los Angeles CA:

Well first off, congrats on penning this verse book Joey! All I can say is anything Joey creates or speaks about truly comes from an authentic place. They broke the mold when you were born and you have achieved more success than most can imagine in a lifetime. You're my brother from another mother across the pond. May you have all the success with this book and many more to come. One love!

Anthony Spado

STEPHEN SAYERS (Staunch and loyal friend to me and my father):

From one author to another I wish you all the luck in world with this book. You're a chip off the old block and your Dad would have been very proud.

CHRISTIAN SIMPSON (Kindred Spirit):

Mr Joe Pyle is not only a very respected individual within the boxing industry on a global scale but he also is a truly gifted writer with the ink of a pen.

Proud to call him a friend for now, well over 20 years.

Wishing Joe, all the best of success with this book of poetry, that will have been written from the heart.

God Bless from Christian Simpson.

ALAN PARAMASIVAN (Always been family & as Old School as they come):

From Villain to Verse... aka 'cheeky wee chappie to poet', and after reading the enclosed you will know it! Trust me, he hasn't gone all soft on us. Far from it, he has quite openly and very frankly and 'at last' put pen to paper allowing us an insight to a very entwined detailed life, following in the footsteps of his late father, in as much as being very respected amongst powerful people in London's underworld as well as being a straight and upfront business, and loving family man. He has many, many stories to tell, some that he can't and others he shares first hand in this extremely clever and entertaining format. Joey Junior aka Joey London has travelled from boxer to now boxing manager, mixing with everyone worth mixing with and will, knowing him as I do, be powerfully successful in the fighting promotional world as well as the literary business bringing you amazing entertainment. If you get the opportunity to ever meet Joey, you will immediately realise he is a man of intriguing depth. That added with creativity and humour allows him naturally to translate his knowledge into story telling. I've had the pleasure of knowing Joey Junior since he was a wee cheeky chap of a school boy, always looking as if butter wouldn't melt with that beaming smile, through his mischievous teenager years ducking and diving all over London and now having joined the adults in the fifties club he is completely focused on giving everything he does true value and significant meaning, all of which you will all now be privileged to witness as he puts pen to paper. His late father was a very, very dear and close friend of mine and I'm certain that he is looking down very proud indeed. To me Joey is family and these my personal comments about him and his work may well be bias but I am a man who doesn't suffer fools and I can, hand on heart, tell you upfront that you will be pleasantly moved with what you are about to read.

Much Respect and Love, your pal Al.

JOCELYN BAIN HOGG (Author of *The Firm* and *Family* books):

I have kind of grown up with Joe. I was there in 1997 with my camera photographing my first book *The Firm* and him being, well him. He's never changed in all these years. Always the same keen intelligence and wry, dry sense of humour. It was great to find someone in that new world who was my age and didn't judge me. Joe was always as straight as it got and that too has never changed. Somewhere Joe has a destiny to fill that is all his own and now is his time: he is a rare one and I am proud to be his friend. I greatly look forward to literally this new chapter.

MICHAEL COLEMAN (The Original Gentleman & one of my dearest pals):

It is with absolute pleasure and an honour to o be asked by my very close and best friend Joe to write a little about him for his new upcoming poem book. I've known Joe a number of years now and can honestly say Joe is a king of kings and born leader. He comes from an extremely highly respected family and after the passing of his father in 2007 has done his late father and all family and friends proud by filling the empty shoes and grasping the reigns tightly.

Joe has a heart of pure gold and is highly intelligent and superbly knowledgeable! He looks out for absolutely everyone and cares deeply and loves all his family and friends. Joe is shown love and respect wherever he goes and is polite and respectful to everyone. However, God help anyone who makes the mistake of trying to wrong him or anyone who is connected to him as Joe will not take kindly to this and they will pay for their mistake! Joe will stand by your side come rain or shine and I will do the same for him and we're all family and hold deep love and respect for each other.

Joe is one of the few old school left now and knew all the fellows and will put anyone right if they're getting their facts wrong and can and does tell so many stories of old and will have you listening like your life depended on it. His humour is second to none and always puts a smile on your face. I'm honoured to have Joe as a best friend and brother and will always love him as such, Michael Coleman

MICHAEL BIGGS (Former business partner & son of legendary train robber Ronnie):

Many years ago on a very private conversation during a so called "underworld" event Joe told me about his poetry, in a macho dominated environment that we where in to have Joe talking to me about poetry was unconceivable. After looking at

Joe for a few seconds to see if he was just pulling my leg I could sense he was trying to reach out to me with a different side of him, this was no longer Joey Pyle Jnr. the son of the legendary Joe Pyle Snr. as I was no longer Biggs Jr.:

We were two fathers speaking of the importance of nursery rhymes and how to educate our children and make them the best literate humans we could, through the love of reading. This was in total juxtaposition with the setting we had around us, of flat-nosed, aftershave-smelling, cropped-headed, hard-looking blokes.

Since that conversation our relationship was never the same, as I have looked at Joe as someone who is more in touch with people's spirituality and what they have to offer. Joe is hardly ever seen to have a softer side to him.

Many who read this may not believe the words above, however, look past the surnames and past histories and they may find that, especially in this case – the book cannot really be at all judged by its cover.

Michael Biggs – March 2017

CREAM (USA Rapper & family to the bone):

I met Joe Pyle around 15 years ago. I had an instant attraction to his aura and his attitude to life. Joe helped me grow as a man and as an artist, and I'll always be grateful for the guidance he has shown me – he took me under his wing like a family member would, and that is what we became...family. His loyalty is 2nd to none, his business knowledge it's fascinating to watch grow. I was born to be by this man's side for life. He has always shown me the real Joe and I wish him the best of luck always. This book will be one hell of a read. Love you Joe.

TEDDY BAM BAM:

Good luck with book Joe, TED!

TERRY BARRETT (Some call him weird but a 'Goodfella-friend of mine'):

The day that I met Joey Pyle,
he had this swagger and certain style,
not sure what I thought at first,
to be honest I thought the worst...

But in time I have got to know,
I hold him high at first was low,
but now weve gelled, he's a super guy,
he's pretty cool he's pretty fly...

I did not know his dad Joe,
the type of guy I would have loved to know,
I missed the boat on that my friends,
and this is where this poem ends....

T. XXX

Introduction

BORN naughty?

Is anyone really born naughty? Can your genes dictate what life has in store for you?

If such a statement is true, then surely, I must come close to the mark. I was born into a family where records can be traced to the Old Bailey criminal courts in central London back to the 1700's!

The first Pyle documented at the Old Bailey was back in 1777 when Paul Pyle was found guilty of stealing handkerchiefs in Paddington. Paul Pyle was sentenced to transportation to Australia. In 1812 John Pyle was sentenced at the Old Bailey for theft with violence and was publically whipped at the corner of Caledonian Road and Pentonville Road in front of a crowd of over a 1,000 people. The following year John Pyle was arrested and found guilty of burglarious breaking into the shop where, like his grandfather, he was sentenced to transportation to Australia for seven years.

In 1857 another John Pyle was found guilty of stealing suet from a butcher's shop and just like his relatives he was given seven years' transportation to Australia.

So, that is just some of my family, just some of the early records we have found but of course I didn't know these men. Let's move forward a couple of hundred years to the turn of the last century.

My grandfather Arthur Pyle was one of five brothers and was also a twin to his brother, Joe. They were born around the Kings Cross area of London which was on the borders of London's East End. It was a harsh area where crime was rife and men had to fight to get any kind of respect.

My grandfather was a quiet man but was very well respected around the cross; he would use violence as a last measure but was very good at winning when it mattered. His twin brother Joe was completely the opposite, he was loud and somewhat flash. When they would go out and do a warehouse or ping a safe my granddad would save his money, whereas Joe would go out and buy a new suit and waste his money on clubs and girls.

It's funny, but many people say that my father Joe Snr took after his namesake Joe while many say I inherited the quiet thinking side of my grandfather.

The love of my grandfather's life, Catherine Gray (my father's mum) was a tough east end woman whose mother came from the streets of Glasgow. My grandmother was the toughest person I have ever known, ruthless in her adoration of her family and couldn't stand outsiders. Some of my earliest memories of her are when she used to say to me, 'Joey, never let anyone take any liberties with you.' Another saying of hers was 'Be wicked! When they know you are wicked then they leave you alone.'

She was from Irish and Scottish catholic heritage and whenever she got the chance she would always sing the Irish rebel songs; Kevin Barry was her favourite song and for as long as I can remember she would sing it at all the family gatherings. It's funny as other kids my age were being taught to sing nursery rhymes like Hickory Dickory Dock, I was taught to sing rebel songs, like 'Shoot Me like an Irish Soldier.' I was a strange up-bringing, a different up-bringing but to me it was normal.

I suppose I was born naughty! It must have been in the genes or something. The saying goes he was a born villain, or a born crook. I was definitely born something like that. I can't see it any other way really. It really was my destiny as sure as I was destined to grow my first tooth.

One thing I certainly wasn't was destined to become a lawyer or a banker or some other nine to five mug (as we called them). I wasn't born into poverty nor was I born with a silver spoon stuck in my mouth, I was middle class, lived in a middle class area, went to a middle class school and had middle class mates. But something was always different with me, I just didn't fit into anywhere. I made plenty of mates as I grew up but lost them as soon as got them when I discovered their morals and ways were different from mine. Morals and codes that were drummed into me from the time I could walk.

My upbringing wasn't particularly hard or strict, but it was very much different. I was taught at school about all the usual educational things but then I had another education at home. It was like a secret society to me, a romantic, fun, forbidden way. Everything about my home life was different from my friends. Their homes, fathers and families were plain, ordinary… boring, My father's family and friends were 'tough guys'. They looked tough, acted tough, drove flash cars, wore flash suits, carried lots of cash and dominated any room they walked into.

I wasn't born the wrong side of the tracks or any of that old bollocks. I can't stand all that crap about how I was born pot less. Sure we didn't have much but honestly, I couldn't give a fuck about what I didn't have. All I cared about was what I was gonna take me.

There were three certainties at my birth. I would break the law, I would go into boxing and I would, at some point, go to prison.

It was the Oxford and Cambridge University of crime

My Nan would say, 'He's a boy! … Boys are always little devils.'

Therefore, it was no surprise I grew into what most people call a rascal. To me it was natural. I was right and everyone else was wrong. I loved the clannish ways of my family, to me they can never be wrong. Even now, where I walk in the world of the businessman, the wolf within can never be tamed.

Rules

Never ask who it was phoning.

Never talk too much.

Leave the room if friends came around.

Mind my own business.

Never repeat anything that I might overhear.

Never ask questions.

In the next few chapters you will hopefully find someone who has strived all their life to break free from the confines into which I was born. This isn't just another crime book. I haven't done large amounts of porridge or been involved in a headline crime. Yes there have many, many times I have broken the law and yes, there has been times I've thought about being what people call a gangster.

But for me my life has been about trying to make it legit, trying to be secure and doing everything in my power to make it other than be a crook.

* * *

Just one moment of madness

Can rescind a lifetime of moments

Intro Two

Joey Pyle – My father

TO write my story I feel I need to begin with a brief chapter about my father. Although there will be many mentions in the chapters ahead, I want to break down some of the myths and try to give you a true reflection of the man. So many things have been written about him over the years – Don of Dons, the Boss, the main man. If you pick up nearly any villain book somewhere inside the book you will come across the name Joey Pyle. Books written by The Krays, Freddie Foreman, Tony Lambrianou, the Great Train Robbers, Paul Ferris, Dave Courtney, Charlie Bronson, Howard Marks, Wilf Pine, Roy Shaw, Lenny McClean, all of their books mention him in some shape or form.

My father passed away in 2007 after a three-year battle with motor neurone disease and there isn't a single day that goes by where something or someone doesn't make me think of him. To me he was my Dad, the man I could trust and the man I admired. In my life, there are only four people who I truly look up to, Jesus Christ – Mahatma Ghandi, Cassius Clay and Joe Pyle.

I am not saying he was a saint or divine, but he was everything I have inspired to be. He was strong, he was fair and for a man labelled as a villain he had an amazing empathy for those who he shared this world with.

My Dad lived in two areas in his life, Caledonian road North

London and Carshalton on the fringe of South London. Over the years, he remained friends with people on both sides of the water. People say he is a hard act to follow but those who say that don't know me or my father. One of the main things he instilled into me is that no man should follow another man, you follow your heart, you follow the way you believe is true. He spent his entire life living this way.

So have I.

Early life and mischief

MY poor mum was over the moon when she gave birth to me in 1967. Tired from the birth she was surrounded by friends and family, all keen to get a glimpse of her new born son. The room was full of flowers and dozens of telegrams, congratulations from around the world. Reggie and Ronnie Kray, Freddie Foreman, even a telegram from the USA which said 'Mazel Tov, Meyer and friends' which was sent from Meyer Lansky and another one from Chicago outfit boss Sam Bataglia.

On the first day of me entering this world I was visited and held by Ronnie Kray. Jack the Hat McVitie, who'd robbed a chemist or something, brought with him half a dozen black sacks full of baby clothes and nappies. Tony Baldesare, a notorious armed robber who was best friends with my father, came to see me as did Peter Tilley, another well-known south London face. Even Oliver Reed, the actor, paid his respects to my arrival.

So, I wasn't even a day old and already I had been held by some of the most fearsome gangsters in London and dressed in stolen clothes!

That night my father went out with his brother Ted and his pals and drank the pub dry, then at six in the morning Dad turned up at the hospital with Peter Tilley and Tony, still drunk and struggling to lift a huge new television they had got as a gift for the nurses.

So, that was first couple of days on this earth. I was too

young to remember of course but one of my earliest memories was a year later when I was on the run! Yes, one-year-old and I was hiding out in Italy with my Mum, Dad, sister, Johnny Nash and his wife and Peter Tilley and his wife.

The reason was because of the arrest of the Kray firm. My father and John were in business with them with different bits and bobs so when the twins were nicked my Dad and John decided to have it away until they found out just what was happening.

That's an old villain way of life, if someone gets arrested who you are close to then you get away until you find out just what exactly is going on. I cannot remember much about it, but my father told me that he and John didn't know at the time if they were going to 'get a pull'. The Kray's arrests was all over the papers and Scotland Yard were really banging the drum about cleaning up London from organised crime, so in their minds it was better to be safe than sorry.

So, one and a bit year old and I was on the run!

Me and well-known London villain Johnny Nash lying low in Italy

Early life

WE moved to a two bedroom flat in Southey Road Wimbledon when I was around seven-years-old. Southey Road was just off the high street and I can remember Mum taking me to the shops and some of her friend's houses.

From what I can recall of Wimbledon I really liked it. I can remember it being very clean and respectable. It was like another world compared to some of the places I had lived like Stoke Newington in the East End and Kings Cross where I had stayed with family in my young life because my father was in prison or on remand. Kings Cross come to think about it was great fun also. The Second World War had finished just twenty-five years or so earlier and much of the East End in those days still had hazardous ground where unexploded bombs lay buried. I remember once as a child when I was staying with my nans sister, Aunt Maggie, me and a couple of pals used to travel the canals down to Kings Cross where we would play in the barren land and explore the dozens of old tunnels they'd there in those days.

One day we found this large metal case at the bottom of an old abandoned building, holes in the roof and everything falling apart. On the ground level there were old bits of wood everywhere and we used to to make a fire. One day when we were ripping up the floor we found this metal case that was three quarters buried in the mud. We found an old rag and started to clean it then discovered there was writing on it. There was an older kid with us, Billy, one of my cousins and he quickly told us all to run. At first, we thought it was the police or the railway security so we just followed and ran till our lungs were bursting. Once we finally stopped I asked my cousin what was wrong and he told us that we had found a doodlebug bomb from the war. We all laughed and I remember making a suggestion that we go back and get it and then put it outside the doors of the local bank at the Angel in Islington. Later that night I hatched my plan and the next day we would borrow my uncle's wheelbarrow and return to the abandoned building to get the bomb. I didn't have a bloody clue how heavy it was or that the reality of three kids picking that up was an impossibility, nevertheless, we were going to get it, take it to the doors of the bank and throw stones at it and hope it blew the bank up, we would then run into the bank, steal the cash and make our getaway to the canals where we knew that no cars could follow us.

That night I can remember hardly sleeping because I was so excited. At around eight in the morning I remember my Uncle Len calling me down the stairs. I walked down and saw that there were two policemen standing in the hallway. My first thought was about the bank job we had planned so straight away I just clammed up and looked at the floor.

Uncle Lenny then looked at me hard and said, 'Where was this bomb, Joey?' I shook my head and said I didn't know. Lenny asked me again and I just said 'I ain't saying nothing!" The policeman then laughed and knelt down, grabbing me by my arm. I can remember his grip was firm but then when I looked up he smiled. 'Look son, you're not in trouble, but we need to send someone in to find this bomb. Someone can get killed if we don't find it.'

I looked up at my uncle Len and twigged that my cousin had told his father that we had found a bomb whilst playing. Uncle Len had then called the cops to report it. Just like any responsible father he didn't want kids playing around where there were bombs.

"Joey, you are not in any trouble, just tell them."

"Why don't you ask Billy, he is the one who told you about it?" I replied. talking about my cousin.

"Billy is at school." Lenny replied

"Well I ain't saying nothing, Nan said never talk to the coppers!" I answered, determined.

"Joey, this isn't talking to coppers, it's just helping them to keep the area safe," my uncle Len said.

"Well I ain't fucking helping them!" I snapped back.

I was then sent to my room and the policemen went to Billy's school where my cousin told them where to find the bomb. Later that night I can remember having a terrible row with my older cousin where I called him a grass and we had a massive punch-up in the room. Uncle Lenny came upstairs and grabbed hold of both of us and I can remember him grabbing me by the scruff of the neck and pushing me onto the bed. He was furious that I called his son a grass.

"Don't you ever say that about family!" he shouted at me.

"Family don't tell tales!" I said back to him.

Uncle Len then sat down next to me and grabbed my hand. He looked at me and told me he knew about my plans to blow up the bank and was trying not to laugh. He then said that his son was not a grass and that he didn't tell the police ,he just told his father about the crazy plan. He wasn't trying to get me in trouble but trying to save my life.

"In my book that's a fucking grass!" I can remember saying.

My uncle Lenny shook his head. Lenny was an old-school villain and was famous in the underworld as being what was called a 'safe-blower'. He was one of the best and he knew the old ways like the back of his hand. Lenny was good friends with my grandfather, Arthur Pyle and together they had 'screwed' dozens of establishments. Uncle Len's claim to fame was being the first man to ever use gelignite to blow a safe in London.

Together with my grandfather they would rob the 'Gelly' from the stone quarries and then use it in their work. It was a very dangerous thing to use, too much and you would blow the building up, too little and you would not blow the safe but make enough noise to alert everyone nearby.

Lenny was not a big man but had a very intense character. He could look at you and without saying a word you just knew that you were in trouble, Lenny grabbed me hard by the face and looked at me.

"You listen Joey, a grass is the worst kind of scum in this world, and you never, ever call someone that unless you know for certain that that man is a grass!"

It's funny but I still keep those words close to my heart and to this day they have never made me wrong. There have been many, many times in my life where people throw cheap accusations around. I don't get involved in gossip. I hold my own views and my own opinions and if anyone ever says to me that someone is a grass then I want to see proof. That way of thinking comes from all those years ago, with my finding a Nazi bomb and my dear old Uncle Len teaching me a lesson in life which had made me some lifelong friendships.

Years later when I was in Belmarsh Prison, I wrote this poem. Some of the other cons copied it out and stuck it on the walls. I can remember the screws pulling me up one morning saying I was causing a disturbance on the wing. I laughed and said that I thought prison was about reform. Well, I am writing poetry so isn't that fucking reform?

The Slag

You sold out your friend to save your own skin
Your name is now soiled to you and your kin
You betrayed the trust; you sold out your soul
Your scheme was successful; you scored your sick goal
No one respects you, even your pals the police
Your life now is running, you'll never sleep in peace
I watched you in court lying to my face
Now I'm in prison, preparing my case
How could you do it? You coward, you rat
You're an insect that's all a bloodthirsty gnat
This is my reward for being your mate
But I'd rather be in prison than have your fate.

One day, one day
What comes around?
Goes around!

I wrote this in Belmarsh prison thinking of the slag Richard Leddingham or Richard Green which was his new name given to him by the law. Remember his name and if you ever meet him, then spit in his eye. He is the lowest form of human being there is.

Prison

IN my life I have worked with many different people and most of their stories will go with me to my grave.

Since I was young, I always had a sixth sense to remain 'one step ahead' so to speak. I lived on the edge for many years but was fortunate enough or clever enough to remain a free man. When the long arm of the law finally grabbed my collar, it was ironically for something I never did!

Now I hear many people saying, 'you got away with this and that' so things just caught up with. 'BOLLOCKS!' I say to that and ask you to imagine this.

Let's say every night you speed home from work and break the speed limit but every night you get away with it. Then one night you drive home, doing 30 all the way and a copper pulls you over for speeding. You ask what's wrong and he says 'speeding' but you reply I've done 30 all the way home. Then the copper replies, yes tonight you did but last night I think you were speeding, so I'm nicking you for it tonight! Let's be honest what would you all say?

You would say ' BOLLOCKS!'

Anyway back to the early nineties and my time in prison.

Believe it or not I was arrested by the regional crime squad for information that linked me with the proceeds of the Brinks Mat robbery. It's a long story but complete cobblers, typical old bill stuff, making up fairy tales.

Anyway on this day I had NINE unmarked police cars following me to a meeting. I arrived and met someone who was working for my father who at this time was in prison. This man was a straight businessman and was weekly giving my mother money which was my father's share of the business. I say straight, but he like most of us had a few rough edges. He knew at the time I was working with people in South Africa, so on the meeting he asked me if they would be interested in counterfeit currency? I said maybe they will and with that he gave me an envelope with £500 of dodgy notes. A few minutes later the window went through on the car and I was dragged out by three armed police, cuffed and thrown on the ground.

They searched my friends car for what I later found out was based on an anonymous 'tip-off' looking for 50KG of cannabis resin. Where they got that info from I don't know, but they found nothing except the envelope of counterfeit notes which was still on the dashboard.

When they found the dosh, I was cuffed lying face down on the ground with some big fat fucker kneeling on my back and a gun pointed in my ear.

Now remember, the man with me was my father's business partner in a legit business company and was giving my Mum money every week while Dad was away. This guy had a financial advisors license or whatever they call it, so I knew if he was caught with dodgy money then his business was over as was the 'bung' to my Mum every week.

Biting my fucking lip and going against everything I have ever believed in, I shouted out that the envelope was mine before they could ask him why he had it in his car.

To be honest it made me feel fucking sick. I had NEVER made a statement or owned up to anything, but this time it involved family so I took the blame.

A few months later I was convicted and sent to prison.

So here I was doing porridge for something I didn't do and

all because I didn't know the fella was turning up to the meeting with an envelope of dodgy notes. I went to see him about a legit PLC company that we were looking at taking over and ended up in Brixton walking out my cell in the morning to the voice of some poxy screw shouting at me to ' DO YOUR FUCKING COLLAR UP!'

Prison really didn't bother me. I was more pissed off with the fact that the old bill had one over on me. I did my time the right way, didn't make any waves and kept myself to myself. I had a couple of rows but then that's what happens when you get thrown into an environment with hundreds of mugs who think they're tough!

I did hate Brixton though. It had a stench about it that was in your clothes, in the food, in bloody everything. I was there for about five days when one night the cell door was opened at around nine at night. Two screws called me and said I had a phone call.

"What do you mean a fucking phone call?" I asked, looking as surprised as them.

"Downstairs, it's your old man on the phone," one of them replied looking proper pissed off.

They led me downstairs where I walked into their office and picked up the phone to speak to my father who was on remand in the unit double Cat A in Belmarsh.

"Joey, you alright son?"

"Yes Dad, what's the matter?" I answered, worried.

"Nothing, we're all here having a protest. We ain't going back to our cells unless I get their word they will bring you over here," he answered, clearly angered. "Now, do what you got to do and we're going to do what we have to!"

Two days later I was transported to the top security prison in the UK, all courtesy of my father and three IRA men who refused to get locked up unless I was moved. At first I was pleased to out of the 'shithole' Brixton. Being in Belmarsh meant

Me and Dad in Kenya. A few years later after this picture was taken we would share the same prison.

I could visit my father on Saturday mornings. When I arrived I was taken to the house block and straight away given a single cell, which is pretty unusual. I was two cells away from an old family friend, Ronnie Fields who was arrested with Charlie Kray. I've known Ronnie for years, so I was given loads of snout, Yorkie bars and a few boxes of Ritz crackers.

I found Belmarsh much easier than Brixton. It was cleaner and the food was a hundred times better, the only downside being I was now in a top security prison where I was a Cat D prisoner. I would have gone to Ford open prison, but because of my dad and his mates, that wasn't going to happen now!

Anyway, when I was released in 1993 I can proudly say I have never been back. Since then I have been a president of a union, a company director of two PLC companies, manager of music acts such as Mark Morrison and Brian Harvey, a film producer, an actor and a boxing promoter and manager. Now I can add author to that list!

If anyone can claim to be 'reformed' then surely I could wear that tag! I have in the past, given speeches to young people on staying 'out of the nick'. I'm not proud of my times in prison but neither am I ashamed. I have no regrets, no remorse and if I'm honest, it was all part of becoming the man I am

There is an irony to this short tale. Whilst I was away the man I was protecting moved house and left the country, thus ceased paying my Mum her money. But I believe I did the right thing and can hold my head up high!

Poetry

Where did it come from?

BELIEVE it or not I first started writing verse to impress the girls. I would send them a small card and put a few words in and because of the success it gave me I must have thought I was good at it. They were short, comical little pieces of rhyme, corny stuff like -

> The next time I meet you can I give you a kiss
> please be generous and don't take the piss
> make my day and don't call me a farce
> kiss my neck and pinch my arse!

It was just a bit of light-hearted fun, a bit cheeky cockney and a bit romantic, nothing serious! I suppose the serious side, or the side of poetry that gripped me, was a few years later when I was unfortunate enough to find myself in the cell in Her Majesty's Prison, Brixton. It was 1992 and in those days, you never had TV's and 'Playstations' in your cell, you had fuck all! Just a pen, paper and time to think about why you were in there. I can remember lying in my cell having just received a letter from Ronnie Kray and at the bottom of the page he wrote a quote from Winston Churchill.

If you're going through hell, keep going

I remember reading that small quote over and over again, writing it out and sticking it above my head on the bunk bed. I found myself saying it loud countless times a day. The next few days saw me get my hands on a book by Lord Alfred Tennyson. That changed my life – the words and the way he put them together just blew me away. The man was an absolute genius in literature. It was funny, but up until I started reading his stuff I didn't know men like this existed. I looked up to crooks and famous boxers and thought all pen-pushers were mugs and less than the men I knew. Tennyson, however made me look at life from a different perspective. He made me realise that some of the things going on in my head were not a form of madness, but an acceptance of my passion, loyalty and strong morals. Below are a couple of verse he wrote and the ones that really hit home with me.

Ring out the false, ring in the true

And out of darkness came the hands that reach thro'
nature, moulding men

Knowledge comes, but wisdom lingers.

Guard your roving thoughts with a jealous care, for speech is but the dealer of thoughts, and every fool can plainly read in your words what is the hour of your thoughts.

No man ever got very high by pulling other people down. The intelligent merchant does not knock his competitors. The sensible worker does not knock those who work with him. Don't knock your friends. Don't knock your enemies. Don't knock yourself.

Lord Alfred Tennyson

They are just a few examples of Tennyson's work, the words of a genius! As I read more about him I found myself exploring his soul, realising he was putting down on paper his wisdom and words from somewhere very deep. I found myself being in awe of the man. I also found myself believing that I was, in some way, a kindred spirit of his.

Suddenly everything was opened up for me. The confined ways of my youth were blown open as I discovered a side to me that had been locked away under years of blindness.

If I'm honest, it's the short quotes that I truly love. I love long poems, but try not to confine myself to any formula. I believe poetry comes in all guises to the point I believe poetry cannot be regulated or confined. That is what makes it powerful, makes it special. The ability to be free from any boundaries. Poetry for me is the heart speaking on paper; a thought or passion put into words. It is mankind's finest achievement in the literary world, better than any novel or epic masterpiece.

Poetry is natural, pure and born from passion. Whether that be great hate or great love, poetry can never be denied.

I feel the blood pump through a broken heart

Yet my will and my thirst for love remain

I am a man... A MAN full of life

Full of passion and full of compassion

I have only one life... I will live it my way

I will feed from my feelings and if I am different... then so be it!

I am free... FREE!

Joseph Pyle

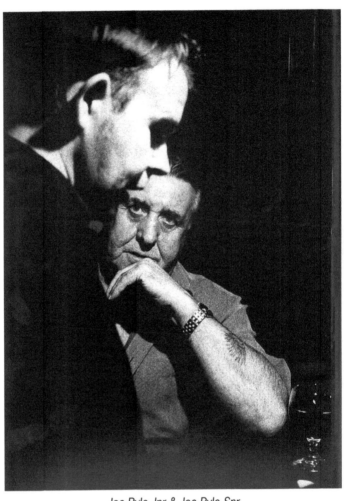

Joe Pyle Jnr & Joe Pyle Snr

Picture credit: Jocylyn Bain Hogg

Poems

by

Joseph Pyle Jnr

To break into the establishment first you have to look and see
what they are doing.

Study how the got there and decide how to better it.

Don't copy don't ask

Force the fucking door open

People on the top of the hill become complacent

They sit and take a breather and pat themselves on the back

The predator is coming

He grits his teeth with determination as he pushes himself

The top of the hill is in sight, we can hear the voices above

They are there but I am coming

I come battered and bruised but there is no turning back till I
reach the top

Make way, make some space, welcome me

Or once I get there I will simply throw you off the fucking top!

Joe Pyle Jnr

The Path

By Joe Pyle Jnr

Every now and then we come to a crossroads in our life, a time of great contemplation where we must choose a path to proceed. Do we stay on the path we know? The path that has become tiresome and predictable, or do we take the unknown path?

Do we rid ourselves from the baggage of life, the same weight that has now become almost unbearable to carry and seek out new ideas and new challenges, or stay the same?

Stay on the same familiar path that we have walked upon for most of our lives; continue into old age walking safely upon ground already trodden.

Life can play funny games with you, you may already be frightened for what lays ahead, worse you may be dreading what lies ahead, yet still we continue to walk hand in hand with familiarity, and still we repeat what we did yesterday.

Amongst all this fear time passes by, another day, another month, another year. Slowly it takes pieces away from you, as we grow old we begin to lose those who we love, we lose our parents and those who we once called close friends disappear as our paths drift apart. Our health and vitality drift away, the energy we once had slowly ebbs into decisiveness, we question if we have the time left to complete what we once dreamt of.

Every morning before our eyes we see our face another day older, our dreams another day lost.

Every day the unknown path feels more frightening, the heart says yes and the mind says no!

Personally, I thrive on new challenges, I need them or I feel like I am dying.

It is the unknown that brings me to life; it fills me with youthful optimism and inspires the soul of a poet in me.

So just do it! Just go for it!

If your life has come to a standstill and you ache for new adventures, then throw off your confines and take the new path.

Whatever happens, you would have added to your experience of life and if it doesn't work out then all you have lost is endless familiarity and a dreary race to your grave.

I want to Live

I want to fly…

No longer will I sit in darkness and hide among these walls

I want to unleash the life within, bring the world into my life.

Grasp life by the throat and squeeze what I want.

Rid myself of the fears and negativities and fly on the hopes of freedom and beauty.

No longer will I fear what will happen.

Grasp this life and fly with hope in my heart, enthusiasm and joy as I look at the sunshine through eyes of optimism.

No more hiding in the shadows scared that I may make a mistake.

To hell with them…I will live!

Live as a free man…live as a human being, full of love and passion.

I will throw off my chains, rise from the confines of pressure and doom.

I have one life and I will live it.

My will and zest must break free, now is the time, no more waiting.

Fly...fly... and find my worth, it is there ... buried in chains of baggage.

Buried by those who fear me being so free.

I want glens and meadows of sunshine, the feel of a warm breeze on my brow and the feeling of satisfaction that when my time is finally over I can say I did everything I could to live my life to its full.

Today I rise from a huddled position, frightened to be seen... today I stand and open my arms and smile as I smell the world...today I embrace life...today I begin to live.

Wrath

Blow your battle horns and stoke your fires,

A dawn of vengeance is coming,

A time of change is approaching like a tsunami crashing against the land,

I smell the fear in you and feel your confusion,

You have made me,

You have created your own doom,

There is no stopping me now; I come for you and your life.

Everything you knew will now come crashing down,

You pushed too far, you laughed too much,

I was content to live, but you were not content to leave me alone.

Now I come for you with all of my power,

The power of one who can take no more,
A lifetime of constriction will soon be released upon you,
It will be like a volcano as I explode my anger upon you,
You cannot defend such angst,
You are now on the precipice of destruction,
You have sowed the seed of your own oblivion.

A Friend in need is a Friend indeed

What is a man when he has won and lost?
A man who is staunch, no matter the cost.
A man who is strong, a man who is fair
A man who can love, a man who can care,
To be a friend, to be a mate
When you are in trouble I'll never be late,
A man you can trust, I am your friend
Behind your back, I'll always defend,
I'm always here and have your back
When you are wrong I will pull you back on track,
Advice I give will always be true
For it is only suggested for the love I have in you,
I'm a man of the past, a relic of time
I am what I am, no matter the crime,
I'll be here for you no matter the test
Cos the morals I have are simply the best,
Don't judge my life, judge how I live
Ignore all the rumours and see how I give,
I'm just a man, made from simple flesh and bone
But my ways and my soul are mine to own,

To be my friend you have nothing to fear
Because when trouble comes your way, you know I'll be near,
I won't run away, I won't look to hide
I have too much loyalty too much pride,
So, you be the judge and you decide
Do you want me with you and by your side,
Cos when the bullets fly and others run
I'll be the one pulling a gun.

My Sons

Stand tall, walk proud
Never too brash or never too loud
Lead from the front, lead as you live
Be wary how you take and wise when you give
Protect your honour and stand by what you trust
Even if it means returning to dust
Watch your words closely, never barter with talk
It is stronger to listen than join the walk
Be vigilant to lies, see through their verses
Judgement is silence than deal in curses
Silently study the ways of the weak
Then trust in you view and let your heart speak
Never be prudish, be open to all
Yet know the decision is yours to call
Be confident in your body, be solid, but care
The greatest of men is the one who is fair
If you are challenged with uncertainty, then take a retreat
It is better to think than rush to defeat

Remember my son to use your head wise
Never be bitter never show despise
Compassion and empathy are what makes you strong
Helping first will never make you wrong
Live your life free and don't hang your head in shame
You have a duty to your children who will carry your name
When all seems lost, you must reach within
Sometimes it will be hard when it's easier to sin
But remember your background, and who you are
Know that my love will never be far
You will soon be a man with the world as your stage
So live it free and not in a cage
The worst kind of prison is the one in your mind
Walk past your fears and never look behind
It is your life to live so you live it free
Be yourself for all to see
The most precious of gifts is my advice to be true
But it is your life my son and yours to do...

Sonny Joe, Cassius and Manny

Its... On!

I cannot eat, I cannot sleep
Don't have time to sigh and weep
They're coming for me, they are on their way
This is my life, just another day
They told me there are armed, they carry a gun
Bullets are gonna fly, back at you my son
You think I am afraid, you try to scare
You picked the wrong man, I just don't care
Drive by shooting! Spray your burst
You better prey and beg I don't see you first
So, we're going to war, we're going all the way
It's my turn now, you have had your say
You called me on the phone and said I am dead
As soon as you see me, I'm getting one in the head
So now you're committed, you must carry out your threat
But believe me you fool, you shouldn't have taken this debt
If you think I'll back down, you're in for a shock
I come from staunch, solid, unafraid stock
You're now in the big league, there's no turning back
If I were you, I'd hit the road jack
You have given me no option, pushed me against a wall
Now all I can do is fight and stand tall
If you're gonna kill me, then you're getting it first
Rather than die, I'd rather be cursed.

Rouse Yourself

Rouse yourself
As did the former lions of your blood
Discover the grit that belonged to your grandfather
Furry the brow and breathe a deep
Clench your teeth as you stiffen with pride
All that you wish is yours to take
You are my king, their king
The king of the world
Let no man utter indifference
Before you I kneel as others do wish
For you my liege we will shake the heavens
Do not hither with time
For the time of your merit has surely arrived.
Let those who scorn, now shake in fear
Let those who conspire, be fearful of the night
Rouse yourself, my majestic of majesties
Rouse your lions and unleash your kingdom
The time for destruction has come
The time of your wraith sits impatient at the door
Let those who scoff, cower in fear
Let those who oppose be driven to dust
Now my liege, the legacy of your ancestor's rests in your
regal hands
Make them proud, take back what was theirs
And in doing so send the starkest of messages
Let no other king sit on his throne unless allegiance is offered.
Rouse yourself my liege
Rouse this nation that stands before you
On bended knee, I beg of thee
Let all and sunder see your mightiness.

Locked away

When you imprison a man, you free his spirit
You lock his body away behind a wall
But you create a feeling with so much more power
Nothing is as strong as a man wanting to be free
You create a resolute hatred of what you do
This man will detest you...he will do whatever it takes to free his body
Even if freedom is gained by death
You lock a man away, you lock away yourself.
The time has come for us to look at who we are.
Are our children to be slaves like us or will they live their lives as free men and women.
The decision is 'ours,' gentlemen.
Either we act or we crawl back under the rock we have been living under for far too long.

The Eagle

The eagle flies high above their heads
Below him are the ravens and crows
As time goes by the eagle befriend the birds flying below him.
He flies above them every day and they are of help to him as they show him where to find food
As the eagle swoops he captures his prey and shares what is left with the crows
At first all is well until the crows start to wish they were eagles
They bicker and become resentful; they pretend they are friends with the eagle just so they can take what they can.

Soon the eagle begins to see their betrayal, he is too wise not to,

Below him the crows are scheming and trying to find ways to copy the eagle

But the eagle just looks, he laughs to himself as he knows he doesn't need them.

He befriended them because he wanted to, not because he needed them.

The eagle then tries to remind the crows that they are just crows, he swoops above their heads at blistering speed where he shows them his magnificence, he even captures another prey and allows them the fruit of his deed, just in the hope they can remain friends.

But there is no stopping the crows now, they are full of envy and greed, they are no longer interested in friendship, all they want is to be, is the eagle.

The eagle has two choices; does he swoop and attack the crows that have grown fat from his labour and show them that can never be what he is?

Again, the eagle is too wise for this, why should he attack and risk injury, why should he lower himself to attack the crows who exist in the sky below him.

The eagle needs no one, he will just fly away and find somewhere else to feed and in doing so he sends a stark message to the crows......

You are all just crows, and that is all you will ever be.

Breaking Bread

I don't know if you know how the world works?

Maybe you know how your world works, but let you tell me how my world works.

Firstly, you come into my company and we break bread, from that crust I let you break bread with a contact of mine. Then behind my back you put your knife into another loaf.

Together you take a bite, together you share the bread behind my back ... now not one of you think, maybe Joe would like a piece of bread. We are both here at this table because of Joe, should Joe not be privileged of this meeting?

Now let me tell you about my world... I live in a world where I trust my friends, when I break bread between us I expect us to share. I don't expect to share my loaf between two friends only for them to meet another day and hide their bread from me.

Is that the action of a friend, or is that the action of someone who cares not for my friendship?

Now in my world if someone is taking from my table and then not sharing from theirs then such an action provokes a response. How should I react to someone who feeds from my goodwill only to hide in the shadows and betray my kindness?

What action should I take? Shall I let that man redeem his action, or should I condemn that man without retribution, should I take him into my world and give him the flip side of my friendship....

The Coward

I will do everything in my power to ruin and scold your deed
There will be books written of your cowardice, scholars will
speak your name in lowered voice
Men will scorn you till the end of time; men will lay shame at
your blood
There will be no grave for your bodies to lie
No words said over your dead bodies
Just scorn and hatred, an eternity of detestation
Revulsion, dishonour, infamy and abhorrence
That is your reward for this wicked deed on this day.
Take these forth and dispose them to their fate
Shame, eternal shame.

Poor

When you have lots of money, all seems fine
Everything's gravy and fine cultured wine
You walk with cockiness, speak fast and brash
Gloating around with pockets full of cash
But something is lost; you take your eye off the ball
Ignorant your next step could end in a fall
Blinded by conceit, you lose your will
Walking on air, forsaking your skill
Flash cars and suits but something's amiss
Ambition fades as you walk in the midst
Am I still free, is this what I choose
I'm much more alive when I have nothing to lose.

Cannot stop me

Cannot stop me, cannot piss on my spirit
Never, no matter what I keep moving forward,
Sometimes it's like I am running a race in concrete boots
Every step kills, every step rips my flesh from the bone,
But I grow more fucking flesh, I never tire, I never give up
I will move forward, I will overcome all your fucking obstacles,
Shoot me, stab me, slander me, try whatever you fucking like
With every fucking act of betrayal, I will haunt you more,
With every barrier, you push at me
I grow stronger and more determined,
I never stop coming forward, I will never be beaten
Even in my grave I will haunt your memories,
Even in death I will cast a shadow on your life
I will embarrass you, make you question your manhood,
Destroy you from your own actions; you will burn in my glory
Combust in my wrath, cower from my reputation,
A man is a fucking man in any world
I am just me and that is a man, a man of feeling and principle,
When you are dead and gone, you are buried in history
When I am dead and gone, I am revered in history,
People don't remember money they remember principle
They remember a man who lived and died for what he
believed in,
They remember someone they know they can trust; someone
they know they can rely on.
Do whatever you fucking want
I have already seen it, planned for it and pissed on it,
Whatever happens I keep moving forward.
I never stop, never, forget fucking flesh and bone
I live by my spirit, live by my heart.

Passion

Everybody's hero! When I am gone, they will remember me

They will remember the way I lived and the way that I gived.

NEVER again will I ask for help, never again will I bend on one knee and swallow my pride

I am what I am, full of fucking passion and full of life

To turn your back on me is to turn your back on truth

Never again will you find that truth

A man willing to die for you, willing to go where others will not go

But I will remember and I will use it to once again fly to the heavens

I will crush all before me with glory

Men will curse themselves every morning of their lives that they let such devotion walk away

I am what I am and that is truth!

I am real, truth and something which only comes from the soul

I pledge this passion that I will once again burst from the flames and rise in splendour

Forsaken but still proud,

Only fools cannot see such worth.

Do you fucking know how much pain it caused me to bend on one knee?

Can you fucking contemplate how embarrassing that was?

I knelt with a hand of friendship, then rose with a look of despise

I slowly rose and hid the tears and then took a solemn vow make you so regret your decision.

Now it is my addiction, my journey to break your fucking hearts

To turn your back on me cannot hurt me, it cannot destroy me

What it does is show me your value of me

And be rest assured I am coming for you, be assured I will show you the errors of your ways

I will break every sinew and vessel in my body to crush your foolishness

I would kill for you! ... What is the flip side of that? What is the flip side of such passion?

Please joke, please mock! Please shrug your shoulders, please pay no attention.

I want you not expectant; I want you not valuing me, for you are not my friend

You chose not to be and now a wrath more powerful than anything you have seen is unleashed

I am the proprietor of your fucking doom.

Enjoy what you have and I don't give a fuck about giving you fair warning

Because by turning your back on me you have set into motion a chain of events which nothing can stop.

The Law

The laws of this once great land were written quiet in vain
For there are certain individuals who fail to follow the grain.
The pitfall is punishment if captured committing a crime
The burglar, the blagger, they're gonna get some time.
But if a copper does a crime and is unlucky he is caught
Then why are there no charges on him, are ever brought.
Scotland yard's a joke .... They're rotten to the core
A haven for bent coppers, well above the law.
How many more times are we gonna hear a case

Coppers telling lies, corruption on their face.
We all know of their reluctance to bring their own up
on a charge
Just internal reprimanding, bent copper still at large.
So, if you wish to be a villain you should become a copper
For they're the bastards with a license
to do it good and proper.

Life is too short

Life is too short to pretend
I live in a life where I mix with street and politicians
I am what I fucking am, just me,
No pretend, no trying to be something I am not
Just a man, a friend and a man who lives with no bosses
I trust my heart, live by it, trust it,
No matter what, I will not change
No matter what comes my way I am what I am,
I wear my heart on my sleeve, I can't help that, I live life,
Life doesn't live me,
I breathe freedom,
I cannot be someone else,
I look in the mirror and see me,
I see someone who embraces the romance of being
Injured, cut, bruised,
Yet still the same, nothing can alter that
My kin lived for me to be me
For me to be just a man,
Just a man who wants to live life pure
No fucking betrayals, no fucking back stabbing

I am too proud for that, too bound by my honour
Take it or leave it, I am me,
Just a man... a man who lives by my heart.

Nothing to Lose

When you have lots of money, all seems fine
Everything's gravy and fine cultured wine
You walk with a cockiness, speak fast and brash
Gloating around with pockets full of cash
But something is lost, you take your eye off the ball
Ignorant your next step could end in a fall
Blinded by conceit, you lose your will
Walking on air, forsaking your skill
Flash cars and suits but something's amiss
Ambition fades as you walk in the midst
Am I still free, is this what I choose
I'm much more alive when I have nothing to lose.

Ode to the Somme

The sun has set and now the horror of the night begins
I look around in our trench, our trench filled of mud and blood
besides me stand the men who I call brothers
We live together, fight together, die together
Last night we lost Martin... a bullet just below the eye
Silence then the terrifying sound of a sniper's rifle
We duck down and then next to us we hear the thud
The thud of a brother
Life gone in an instant.

We turn with mixed emotion, for a brief moment we thank god it wasn't us

Then the horror hits home, the horror of another good man, another brother lost to this soulless war.

Maybe tonight a sniper's bullet will seek me

Maybe tonight it will seek the brother standing next to me

We question our sanity every moment of every day

One moment we hope it will be us next, the next moment we prey we will make it home to our families.

Tonight, I will look to avenge my brother, again just like the night before.

Looking out into the darkness, waiting for another sniper's bullet

This is the reality of where we are, we cannot see where the shots are coming from

We only know they will come.

A whistle blows in the distance; we look at each other knowing that many men will fall

Advance! The sergeant screams, advance! As the sound of the Gatling gun fills our souls.

If I ever make it out of this hell hole, that sound of death, the Gatling gun will forever ring in my ears.

I stand hear wet, cold, terrified but I grit my teeth for Britain!

I am a British man through and through and this is my duty

If tonight it is my turn to fall, then let my family know that their father, son and brother has fallen for the empire.

I have met my maker with a Lee-Enfield in my hand and a heart full of pride that I was here fighting for what I believe.

The mud is up to my knees as a rat scrambles past me, six months ago, I would have jumped in the air, now I just smile as they walk amongst us

The horrors of this trench are truly unimaginable, yet there is now nowhere I would rather be,

Besides my brothers, dressed in the uniform of my King,
fighting the fight of the righteous.

If I die tonight, then maybe I have merited that right

Let me take that bullet rather than it let it strike my brotherFor
god, the king and my empire

But most of all, for the man who shares this hell besides me.

King or Fool

I created my demons, I cast the mold

Lived with a heart, soulless and cold

The life of a villain, a life of pretend

Couldn't care less whose life I would end

I sat at the top and destroyed those I knew

Never trusted anyone ... spoke only to few

The blood on my hands was not from my skin

The tears on my cheek were not for my kin

To some I was terror, to some I was god

Ruling my manor with a cruel iron rod

I robbed for money, stole from whoever

Take-take-take was my only endeavour

But what did I win? What glory can I claim?

Scars on faces and hands that maim

Standing in pubs, suited to the nines

Any late payments I dished them all fines

Stoic, hard, dealing in pain

Crushing the feelings of those in vain

But now I am older, repentant and wise

But I look at life with tear glazed eyes.

What I am

My determination shall neither writher nor bend

Instead it shall draw strength from your mocks

Resulting in absolute success, so I invite your jestful remarks

For their spoken word inspires me to spit back those
conceited and

Foolish words that were once uttered to me

For I am a man who dances with ambition and those who
once mocked me with doubts to inflate their own egos and
importance shall one day

Scream with grief and rue the day that they spoke so selfishly
to me

As I grow older and my power grows, I shall remember my
friends and

Equally my foes and my justice shall be wielded on both

The man who crosses my path shall meet with only two fates

Joy or pain with each gift given to their extremes

My hands carry sin and my heart carries grief and my body
carries

Neglect and abuse

Scar tissue in abundance with every scar bearing its own
painful tale

But my head carries hope and determination, passion and
romance and a

Strength that shall take me to the forever-ness of ....
the stars.

Blood-Stained Throne

I've seen men who should be patient acting in haste
I've seen a man stick a blade down another man's face
Sometimes I wonder on our crazy race
I've seen lots of rip-offs' experienced the cons
Wondered of the winners and what they have won
I've tried to decipher what life's all about
But always my conclusion is an anger to shout
It seems we are living a life full of lies
One that doesn't care if our brother dies
One, which is stained by the filthy hand of wealth
One where we joke at another's ill health
It seems now we all know too much for our own good
Once upon a time men knew where they stood
Now we all want which have only the few
An idiom in life which is hardly new
But once we were destined from our place of birth
With our family and friends, we all knew our worth
We accepted our lives and got on with living
We all helped our own and lived our lives giving
But now born a man filled with anger in his breed
Caring for himself is his only need
The tools he embraces are jealousy and pain
He is ruthless, cunning, greedy and vain
He wants to succeed in a world of success
He will tread upon anyone as he strives to be best
What is a man when he stands alone?
Arrogantly sitting on his blood-stained throne

So insecure in his make believe life
Boosting his ego giving other men strife
Choking on the fumes of the power he needs
Ruining lives as his pocket he feeds
Wearing his crown pretending that he's king
Constantly dreaming of what more wealth will bring
Live all your life hurting your brothers
Paying no regard to the feelings of others
You think your superior because you have money
But to those who can see, your wit is not funny
But one day like us you're going to die
Then you'll answer to god for living your lie
But then it's too late, there is no return
The price of your wealth is a destiny to burn!

Bested but not Beaten

Shackled to a chair gasping for air
Blood on the floor waiting for more
Now all alone I am hurt to the bone
Yet inside I smile
Day after day they have tortured my body
Still I am strong I have given them nobody
Cut with a knife and beaten with a stick
Russian roulette as I hear another click
Haven't seen the sun for days on end
Yet its warmth shines brightly as my honour I defend
Tell me the names of the men you protect
Punch after punch only strengthens my reject
Yesterday I was close, close to confess

Today I am past the limit, I couldn't care less
You have played your hand and given me your best
I have now come through your barbaric test
You didn't break me on the first day, now your methods have failed
The more you hit me just makes me more proud
I won't give you anything, only my scorn
Any hope you had is now forlorn
Take off my blindfold; let me see your eyes
I can taste your frustration as yourself respect dies
Hit me, strike me, let me feel another blow
But your never force me to tell you all I know
I am willing to die and go to my grave
With a smile on my face knowing friend's I have saved
Let them live long and let them be free
Let them remember the friend in me
I will rise into heaven with my soul complete
You have taken my life but yours is defeat
Open your arms to me Jesus my lord
I went out fighting holding my sword
So, who has won and who has lost
You can have my life but at what cost
You tried everything you knew to make me talk
Now get out of my way and let me walk
You're a coward, a rat, a man full of doubt
Look at me now as pride I shout
Just walk out the door and leave me alone
I am stronger than you though you've bled me to the bone
Doesn't matter anymore, anything you do
I'm willing to die as long as I'm true
You smashed me near death now you know your mistake

Two men in a room, only one man is fake
I've took your blows and took your threats
And all that you have done is learned regret
The only thing left is you'll hear me rejoice
Defiance and pride are filling my voice
I see your anger I smell your hate
But I'd rather die true than have your fate
I have won, you have lost
Now walk away and remember the cost...

To stand and not crawl

I feel the blood pump through a broken heart
Yet my will and my thirst for love still remain
I am a man...A MAN full of life
Full of passion and full of compassion
I have only one life...I will live it my way
I will feed from my feelings and if I am different... then so be it
I am free... FREE!

Integrity

To go against everything that you know
And not be afraid of fear to show
To refuse what is good for you and accept which is bad
When all common sense is calling you mad
To reach deep within and grasp which is right
To stand up and be counted though no solution is in sight
To stick by your honour when you know it means pain
To show perseverance when they call you insane
To feel content when you're cast out alone

No one's as lonely as a king lost his throne
To start at the beginning when your achievements went far
And hide the secret that your soul is so scarred
To lose everything that you have ever known
Be proud of your nakedness, honour flesh and bone
Your flesh may be bound but your soul remains free
It's how deep you look as to how far you see.

Father

I see my father when I look at my reflection
I see his smile, I see his eyes
As a tear falls I see his love
As my brow furrows I feel his compassion
I swallow deep and think of things I never said
My lip trembles and I sense his soul
He lives in me and in my sons
Every day if I look hard he is with me
In my blood – in my bones
In my heart and in my dreams
How I miss the pat on the head,
The hand on my hand
And the occasional embrace
If I try hard I can hear his voice
It is my voice now
His mind Is my mind
Just one more smile father
Just one more tear
I am your son and all your hopes
Now you are gone – I am no longer the son
I am the father now.

Pressure

When you live on the other side of the fence, everything is magnified by the hundreds, you hear people say about pressure and I wonder if some people have actually looked up the meaning of the word. You hear stories like Nick Leeson was under pressure, please! Robbing millions and millions of pounds, yeah right pressure! That to me is like winning the lottery, I would be having the time of my life.

Then we see that the England football manager is under intense pressure, of course he is! It must be driving him mad wondering where and what to spend his six million pound wages on.

To us pressure is fighting for your fucking life!

Pressure is when you have to move out your family and go to war because someone is coming to do war with you.

Pressure is about making the right decision, a decision squeezed between going to prison for life or catching a bullet in the fucking eye.

Our life is glamorous but so it should be as there are not many who can survive it, pressure is about trying to get out of something all your life when you know it is the one thing you are best at.

They say live by the sword and die by the sword, that is a great saying but to us it's a fucking stark warning, almost a premonition, a reality we strive daily to avoid. Now that's fucking pressure.

Sorry but I must Go ...

I am leaving

So sad but I have to go

I am ripped apart here. You have stabbed me in the heart too
many times

I must take flight and fly away to ventures new

I will take what I have and live my life

You have taken enough of my energy.... taken enough of my
life

Tore the flesh from my soul

Made me question my sanity... made me question my integrity

Only when I am gone will you realise your actions

Only when you fall and you see there is no one to pick you up
again

And if there is what toll will they ask

I gave for nothing

I was yours, your rock, your crutch... the one you could rely
on

Now that's gone...you betrayed yourself

Goodbye my friend... I forgive you and I will cherish the
moments we had

But I am sorry I am too full of passion to be used anymore

I took so much pain...so much agony...dreaming of
something that never existed

I am leaving... I have to go

I am too alive to stay.

Constrained

The concrete castle of your mind
confined, restricted, utterly blind
you fester and fidget, you scheme and plot
constantly cursing of what you have not
fuelled with bile, jealousy and greed
fooled into believing its vengeance you need
you constantly worrying what others are feeling
tales of success send you reeling
totally driven with envy and spite
you've forgotten reality, forgot what's right
choosing to live in the shadows of others
hating success from the sons of mothers
angered, enraged, full of hate
why have you forgot, you have your own fate
your up-tight and squeezed, bound in barbed wire
eyes of greed burning with fire
Tin pot Hitler, cursed in your own dream
bitter and twisted, planning your scheme
your mind has trapped you, imprisoned your heart
but you must break free, find where to start
only you can break yourself free
only you can accept it is me
forget what's expected and live life true
you're limping through life with only one shoe
try to relax and just have some fun
rid this angst of what others have won

Had Enough

I will tear this pain away
I refuse to be confined by it anymore
Like the phoenix, I shall rise from this den of lies
I will rise from within
I will stand erect and spit my defiance as I use it to move on
No more. No more can I be involved
No more can I be used
No more can I have my heart broken
No more.... can I fool myself
You have taken your pound of flesh
Cashed in your 30 coins of silver
My life is now my own... from your deceit you have given me
freedom
I AM free... free from the burdens you placed on me
Free to live once again
Free to be myself
Free to embrace my life again
FREE to breathe...free to exist.

Twas the day

Twas a day where fate appeared
In the midst, I could feel this was the day where my name
would be born
If I live or die, today I will be membered
God give me the strength to be just
Guide my heart to truthfulness
Do not let temptation divert my worth

Let me be strong, for those who follow will have to live with
my actions
Those who I face I face without feeling
Only what I must do, not what I want to do
Today is the day I am willing to die
Please god let it be for the common good
If I am a fool, then make my death come swift
If I carry your word, then guide my will for your salvation
Only truth and justice can I be strong
Only from sufferance can my legacy be revered
Today I give you all I am
Today I stand tall or fall proud
Make my life worthy of your teaching
Make my day, a day of pride
For when all is forgotten and all are long gone
It is truth that shall live through all eternity.

The Critic

He prowls on the keyboard waiting to pounce
Your hard-earned work he is going to trounce
He will tear you shreds ruin your page
He is big-headed and bitter, the computer his stage
Doesn't care if he injures or care who he hurts
His swansong in life is dishing the dirt
Too self-interested to worry about others
Sons, daughters, fathers and mothers
What kind of person wants to belittle?
Must be a person whose life is so brittle

He believes he's superior, oh what a fool
Harming others is not very cool
Don't you realise how much pain you cause
Is there nothing between your ears that makes you pause?
Why do you do it?
What good does it achieve?
Do you think you are clever, is that what you believe?
Are you a person; is there a beat in your chest?
Tearing at feelings, is that your best?
I can't understand, your life must be so sad
What insecurities makes you so bad?
Maybe I am crazy and put faith in all men
Only to be disappointed again and again
The reviewer on amazon, a home of the bitter
As bad as the trolls on Youtube and twitter
Do you feel better now you've had your say
You feel all important as you ruin someone's day
So well done, hope you feel proud
Had your rant and done it so loud
But remember this saying and remember it well
Remember it when your head starts to swell
A little man may criticize
It takes a man with a big heart to sympathise.

The Heart as One

The language of the heart
How is it understood, so many times it falls on deaf ears?
So many times, it is just walked on by
Take the time to listen… take the time to feel

Listen… don't just hear
See the pain in my eyes and see my actions
Inside I am pleading, begging for you to understand
I want you to live… I want you to feel the passion
Embrace it… fall in love with it…live your life with it
I am dying inside, being this alone
As one we are unbeatable
But only when we look at each other with the language
of the heart.

A Friend

Did they expect us to show them respect?
Prove your worth first
Show your friendship
Earn my love
Then… just then you will have the best friend in the world
I will stand by you with my life
Even when you stab me in the back I will value my side of what
we had
You cannot even see that when you hurt me you injure yourself
If you can't see what a friend you have in me, then was my
affection wasted
I give you everything I have and you return lies
You destroy your soul when you try to outwit me
I see you… I see everything you do… my silence, as I pray
that I am wrong only fuels your betrayal
Maybe one day you will realise your betrayal
But because I was your friend and I loved you, I pray you
never do

Now I must say goodbye, farewell and good luck
I can no longer live amongst the lies and the festering stench
of betrayal
I will just go my own way....
Again, on my own.

Be a Man

To always stay composed and never lose your head
To keep you're cool even in the hottest situations
Never deal in threats, play your cards close to your chest
Children use threats as toys of their egos
To always imagine what the other man is thinking thus you
Remain one step ahead
Take heed to caution but do not let it be your master
Caution can be your enemy as well as your friend
Family business must remain within
Never use it as a tool of gossip
To always be fair but don't let fairness make you humble
Twist your threats so the listener hears advice
Anger and rashness decays what they set out to achieve
Nothing is settled by anger, and the man you impose it upon
Will only one day seek his revenge?
To always help the needed though only if just
Keep your eyes open to those who need your help most
A true friend will seldom ask for it
To never seek to disgrace or belittle a man
Your own self-esteem will be the most injured
To remember that true wisdom holds the art of reasoning

Animals in the jungle don't reason, kings, leaders and wise men do

Learn how to master this art for it shall never do you harm if used

Sincerely

Never let drink get the better of you, it will only harm outlooks against you and one day you may have to answer for it

Know when to say no though never be prudish or patronising

Never judge anyone by your own standards or look down on them because they do not possess the virtues that have moulded you a man

Never deal in lies, to lie to a man means to look up to him or pity yourself

Be proud in yourself and be strong in your mind

Do not throw apologies around too often, a truly sorry man does not need to apologise

Though always look out for the exception, accidents do happen.

In This Dark Age

This sick world where smiles hide conceit

Where I matter more than you

Where what I possess is the scale that is used to judge

Where sex is no longer privacy

Where it is chic in social get together's to speak of the unspeakable in order to shock... why...who wants to shock!

Bombarded daily by impossible goals, inferiority complexes are rampant

Friends give advice just to boost their self-egos

Politicians lie... what's new... blatant, carelessness, ignorance, and nonchalance

Robbing the robbed when will it stop

The age of idleness, no one wants to try for fear it won't work... what arrogance, what insanity

Everyone's a genius, everyone's a teacher,

Everyone's a star, everyone's a scholar, everyone's a movie star,

How naive you all are

How you build walls around the lives you live

Prisoners of the 90's

The rich, the handsome and athletic is held above the poor the sick and disabled

How shallow you all are

Admiration has evolved into obsession! Crazy!

What sick twisted society evolved from Thatcher and TV

Ignoring family traditions and beliefs and accept the words of some Yankee actor on TV ... what a terrible disgrace you must be in the eyes of your father

But you don't care... caring's in the past, caring's for the weak, the weak are outcasts... why! Why!

Some people are born weak it was a card dealt to them by nature, so how can you criticise these people, what monsters are you if you do

God has been forsaken, who needs god when we have Hollywood!

Respect! What's that I hear you say!

Hidden faces everywhere, shrouded in masks of fear

What a travesty it is that we cannot show our real self's

Why can't we give our love without conditions?

Stick a needle in your arm and hide for a while ... Ah it feels good... You fool!

Destroy the life that your parents created, that's respect

Selfishness! Greed is all you disgustingly think
Some of you out there are good but not enough
Oh, not enough… oh not enough
Mothers no longer teach their children about god
A little girl robbed from the beauty of faith… what kind of
mothers are you?
I have more than you… O' you lucky people! One day as
time flies by your metal will rust your house will fall and your
clothes will rot but what of you spirit what of your soul
Did your flash cars, flash houses, and fancy clothes really
matter?
Richness is the soul and not the hand when will you all
remember again
Has it all gone too far, is it all too late
Where has the gentleman, society gone, the one which we all
adored
Has women's lib destroyed it
Oh, what a terrible shame if such nobility has been lost!

True to my Word

Well, I've had a good run
I've had some great and glorious times
I've seen sights you could not begin to believe
I've felt passion that is eternal
Felt feelings only Gods could feel
It's been my life
I've lived my way without boundaries or your laws
I've felt love few could comprehend
Pride which fills your lives with envy

Money you've only dreamed of

Power that would chill your beliefs

Respect that you sadly never understood

I am a man true to my word .... True to my honour ....
True to myself and the ways of my ancestry

You live your life sheltering under the blanket of cowardice and
betrayal

You walk in the shadows for you are no one

You walk hand in hand with treachery ....You embrace it and
encourage it to fill your own needs

You are without morals

Yes, sir............. Yes, sir ....is all you believe, your life is
truly empty

Your heart is weak

You are men who speak by the foolish word

Spoken by cowards festered with betrayal

What chance has your family got when it is taught by you ......
A conspirator in weakness and betrayal

My family has PRIDE they walk with heads held high ...... For it
is us,

Our kind who are Gods children ...

Men of TRUTH and HONESTY

The Warrior Within

The bravest of men with the ability to be fair

A mind so sharp, so perfectly balanced

The bite of the warrior as he grits his determined teeth

All else forgotten as his sword leaves its sheath

A man who can decide within the blinking of an eye

To never fear that you may be wrong though be cautious while looking strong

Better to do one thing with all ones might than to half-heartedly attempt many feats

To hold his concentration, be focused and composed

When all around him chaos is crashing down

Nothing sways him, nothing influences him, the decision is his as is the time to unveil it

Always be strong though he understands the ways of the weak

Every action can be seen from different angles .... The warrior sees them all

He listens more than he speaks .... Listening is the birth of knowledge

Speaking is its death

One hand for giving, one hand for taking

One eye for looking, one eye for seeing

See what you hear

His spoken word is to promise

For no words of fools ever pass his lips

His smile is a rarity

Spurred only by affection

Eyes of sincerity, innocence and truth

He has no prejudices nor can none affect him

He knows only right from wrong

Always without a thought of hesitance

To hesitate is to trust in the ways of others

Trust only in his inner self, it is the only truth you'll ever know

Hear the word of council spoken by friends and foe

Though never heed their advice, advice is weakness
Patronising fools telling the world of their mistakes
Study their faces as they tell you their weaknesses.

Anger

An emotion so strong it corrodes all the rest
Voice is strained from the pain in my chest
We shout and we scream, we hurt those who are close
Damaging the ones who we love the most
It turns you into someone, you didn't want to be
Someone who is blinded, unable to see
Now I am sorry, sorry again
Sorry for causing so much pain
Why don't I think, before I open my mind
Why do I try to be so unkind
Blood flowing fast, I want to destroy
Rip out your soul, take away your joy
Why do I do it, why try to hurt
Why are my words being used as a quirt?
Now I am calm and not like before
Feeling like a fool for my little war
But can I say sorry, will you forgive
Can you show mercy, live and let live
Can you see past, my contrived lies?
Can you now listen to my desperate cries?
I am foolish and stupid, I made myself weak
Now I sorry with tears on my cheek
If I could go back, I would choose my words well

But there is no return, once you are in hell
Cut off my hand, cut off my arm
Give me the strength for me to stay calm

Just remember the way I lived.

The Day is Mine

Today is the day I will make my mark
Today is the day I will join the greats
Everything I have I will lay on the line
Today I face an opponent who does not respect me
I will show him what a mistake he has made
I will strike harder than ever before
I will lay my life before him and see if he shares the same
heart
With every blow I will summon my soul
With every step forward I will show him my worth
There will be no surrender
There will be no mercy
I will be ruthless
Strong
I refuse to relent
I refuse to be beaten
My heartbeat will sound like thunder
I will roar like the lion
Let this battle be my legacy
Let this day be the day I am measured
Let this day be the day I join the greats

Reflection

So, the dust has settled and once again I have won
Emotionally I am in pieces
I have gone to that place where only few are brave enough
to go
Hung on the cliffs of oblivion
Lowered myself into the clutches of death
Only now can I take a deep breath
Contemplate and sigh as I gasp at my madness
How many more times can escape a glorious death
How many more times can my mind recover from such
gamble
Once again I have returned
Again, another piece of my soul has been ripped away
Another piece of my heart has left me
The look of stern on my face is another shade darker
The look in my eyes another degree colder

Free

I was born into this world chained by circumstance
Born into a way of life not of my choosing
Imprisoned within a body where I was shackled by life
Couldn't break free, no matter how hard I tried.
Now tainted by a mind which is ripped apart
A heart which cries to be free
Am an outlaw or a man who will not kneel down
Am I a monster who will not comply?

How can a man be free?

How can a man live his own life?

I breathe and I live day to day

Yet I question and I doubt

I see life through a mask of un-trust

Looking at everyone with question

Do they love me or love who I am

What am I?

What kind of a man have I become?

I love yet I am afraid to love

I give yet I am wary to give

I trust when I know I should not

A man from a long-lost era

A man who lives life by his heart

I am a dinosaur, lost an age of no romance

Lost in an age of self-importance

When will someone love like I dream?

When will my prayers be answered?

In my past I was a man of the glens

Wind in my hair and freedom in my blood

I made my own rules

I set my own goals

Now it is my curse

Why did I never realise when I was younger?

When will I be free?

When my body is laid to rest

Only then will my soul be free

Only then will I know true peace
My only hope is my sons are spared this legacy
Let them be their own men
Let them live the way they want
I am their father, yet I cannot be their example
It is a pain they should not suffer
A way of life that was mine …not theirs.
Lord, give me the strength to free them from this bondage
Let them be free
Let them live good
Let them live long and happy
Let them never know the burdens I have carried
I love them with all my heart
Let my suppression, be their freedom
Live my sons live and be free…
Do not remember me

The Road to Ruin

It is a path we all know
It is a path we all fear
A path with such lure
Just one step and then it's too late
Strange how we choose to ruin our fate
Like Adam and the apple, we know it is wrong
Fooling ourselves we are robust and strong
We choose to be weak, we choose to fail
The lure of wealth is our holy grail
Take another step and we pause for a thought

It doesn't feel right, we know we are caught
Deeper and deeper we soon become
With every step our humanity goes numb
Greed and power, we slowly advance
We are now entrenched and engrossed in the dance
Must keep going, there is no turning back
We're on the road to ruin

Why Worry

What will happen will just happen
So why spend your days and nights worrying about it
We all try to do the best we can. But still trouble knocks on our door
So, hey! Just let it happen.
Spend today enjoying what you have and not worrying about tomorrow
What can they do anyway/?
Can they take my soul?
Can they take my life?
Only if I give them
I am fed up worrying, tired of trying to second guess all the answers
So damn it! No more will I waste my days fretting and hiding
No more will I try to please those who are my enemy
Do what you want!

My Father

Lived my life under his wing
To me he was everything, my only king
My reason for being, my god and my lord
For him I would die and live by the sword
I have never been me, only the son
Only in his death has my life begun
I yearned for his pleasure, strived for his smile
Scuppered my life and pretended a style
I rose every morning with only one wish
A nod of approval and a fatherly kiss
To me he was everything, my future, my life
The dread of his scowl would cut like a knife
But what of me now, when I am now all alone
Am I worthy or just to sit on his throne
He was a legend, a myth, a man amongst men
Now that I know what I should have known then
He left me alone, to stand on my feet
Told me to fight and not accept defeat
But he should have loved me, for being his son
Not for the man who now all shun
I did what you asked, I followed your ways
Now I am lonely, alone most days
You wanted a prodigy, you wanted an heir
But with all your qualities, you didn't act fair
You steeped me in burdens, handed me the weight
When you should have shown mercy, told me straight
I love you dad, I always will
But you should have gave me the strength to sometimes kneel
What hope do I have now you are gone afar?
How can I live with a heart so scarred?

Truth

An eternity of gratefulness is my reward for the truth

Just one hour of truth, 60 minutes, 60 seconds of pure and innocent absolute truth

What kind of sensations would it send to my heart?

Will it leave me refreshed or thirsting for more?

Just one tiny hour of truth where everything is clear and full of understanding

A million years of questions revealed in an hour

A million years' worth of burdens and aches destroyed by the truth

.

What is the actual meaning of truth?

That which has no questioning

That which has no doubts

Do we ever experience truth................? Pure truth.

Truth bottom line .... Absolute and total

I doubt we ever do...

A Soldiers Doctrine

A Soldiers Doctrine

In a crisis...stay calm

Always strike to kill. A wounded man can still kill you

Wake early and smell the morning, say your prayers and calm your thoughts,

To be rash will lead to failure,

Cherish and protect your fellow soldiers,
Respect and honour the structure of command,
Carry yourself with dignity and pride,
Show obedience when in battle,
As a man, be the example,
Show mercy when the time arises,
In victory show compassion,
A soldier's voice is soft when not in battle,
He is calm and dignified,
Never disgrace your House or Lord,
Have complete duty to the crown

Swing the sword

If death should come – then make it swift
To be spared of this horror would be god's gift
We fight in the sand, make steps in the mud
Scars in our hearts and covered in blood
We swing our swords using all our might
Smoke and blood hindering our sight
I tread on the bodies of those I call kin
Then question myself for doing such sin
If we win we lose but we must prevail
But will I ever lose this guilt or lose my scowl.
Where have I gone?

Why can I not cry?

What stops me from pain?
Why does death not affect me anymore?
What am I becoming?
I want my feelings back!
I want to know what it feels like to show remorse,
I want to know what it feels like to be a man again,
I am hollow now,
I look at myself in the mirror and I see a stranger
I see empty eyes
I see coldness
I see nothing
God help me…save me from myself.

Choices

When another man barks and another man bites
another man runs and another man fights
When some will shout and some will scream
some will do, some will dream
men of all shapes, mean of all forms
some are rebellious and some reformed
those who say yes and those who say no
Those who are ignorant and others will know
those who take and those who give
some who choose chains while others just live.
Those who are strong while others ore meek
some men are quiet while others just speak
men who are calm where others are show haste
some men just eat while others will taste
the world is an arena where some men shine
the world is your oyster but can never be mine

Greed

A man who is content and driven by me
Blind to the world and all who can see
Head in the air brazen and loud
Walking above his own chosen crowd
He seeks to find peace and importance from choice
Only ever interested I hearing his own voice
He walks through the world caring little for his brother
Self-importance ignorant of another
He dreams of more, more than he's got
Blinded by those of which they have not
He has created his kingdom, made his throne
Little does he know he is all on his own
But his pride will not falter, his pride will not bend
Twisted and corrupt, where is the end
He looks down his nose and makes his own claim
Blinded by pride and courted by fame

Poems and Quotes inspired by war and Battle

War

Now pon the time where shivers chill the soul
A twitch on my brow as I look up into the calm night sky
I can hear the sound of calm,
Waiting for the morrow when whistles commence the sound
of guns
Rata-tat-tat, then men start to fall
Men who the night before I called them my brother
In the mud and blood, we try to make sense
Yet what words could aptly describe such carnage
I walk over bodies, limbs and shattered dreams
I fall into warm blood which once filled men's hearts
I feel a thud in my arm which knocks me to the ground
Then the feeling of warmth as my sight turns to crimson
The bang from the impact numbs me for a moment
Before I realise the horror that a bullet found its target
I fall to the ground fearing another round is on its way
Only to see more of my brothers take my place
What bravery they show, what men I stand beside

No matter what I feel I must get to my feet
Together we may find a way to survive this hell
Together we carve our resolve
Together we share a common bond
Together we fight as lions of the British Empire
For King and country flows through our veins
For the regiment and all that went before us
If we fall, then we fall knowing that we join the noblest stock
Go forward and we never stop
Do not shed a tear for us
Hold your head up high and remember us
Be proud of us and know that we are here so you do have to be
With our sufferance, we give you your freedom
With our pain, we give you peace
We are soldiers
We are men of the empire
Men of nobility
Men of war

Today we tasted defeat for the first time,
A sobering moment as we realise the reality what we face,
The council members are inside the tent arguing amongst
themselves,
They are trying to find blame for why we lost the field,
But the truth is more frightening.... We lost because our
enemy fought better than us.
We are now arguing amongst ourselves...we are falling out
and calling each other names.
When I return to the tent I must pull us back together again.
If not.... we will face many more nights like this.

* *

If we are to prevail then we must find a solution to any problem before us.

When we are outnumbered we must find a way to shorten the advantage,

If we face more experience...we must fuel our youth with conviction,

If they have more swords then we must fight with more lustre,

Whatever we come against we must find a way to endure and prevail.

Whatever is needed, cunning...guile...bravery...strength... even foolishness,

That is the art of war...

* *

How it would be so much easier if we could end this war with a single arrow,

A magical solution to end all the suffering,

Then there would no more pain,

No more tears,

No more deaths,

No more orphans,

No more widows,

No more deceit,

But what good would a win be without honour and sacrifice,

A war without heroes and commanders,

Would it be a war worth winning...?

Is our goal victory no matter what?

Or is it just as important as how we get victory?

When all the death and battles are over...what leaders will we have?

What men will come from this war...what monsters will replace the monsters we fight?

When all the fighting is over and the men have returned to their homes and loved ones,

Then it will be the time of the Kings and councils to forge a new world,

What world will they want?

Will greed replace greed?

Will tyranny replace tyranny?

Will power replace power?

Will my war end when this new world is born?

Or will I discover a whole new enemy?

I pray for the sake of my people we find a balance,

Ruthless in battle but fair in peace,

This battle could be one too far...

To find such man is like finding treasure, men will want what they feel they deserve and Regions will be divided and allegiances stretched.

Maybe this will be our finest hour...our finest battle...if we find the right balance then everything we have achieved has been worth it. If not then all we fought for will be wasted.

Trickery and cunning are your colours

We fight with our heads held high

And we die as men filled with pride

With your actions, you have failed already

Whatever happens now...we have revealed who you truly are... cowards

I can smell death in the air today
It hangs above our heads like a message of caution
We have chosen the right ground
We have the prepared well
Why do I feel so apprehensive?
What unknown forces are at conflict in my mind?
Why do I doubt?
I must be strong and confident,
If the men feel my caution, it will spread among them like a plague of pestilence,
Whatever caution I have, I must hide it deep within.

**

Once again, we await the battle.
Once again, we wonder what fate awaits us in the morning.
We have prepared well…we have made plans within plans.
Yet still we are plagued with apprehension.
Still we have the same feeling in the pit of our stomachs.
As I look upon the faces of my warriors.
Which ones will still be standing tomorrow evening?
I see their smiles and their fears on their faces.
Which of you will be rejoicing…which of you will be mourning.
Who amongst you will be still be in the living world.

**

It troubles me that I love the battle.
Can I live without it…I don't know if I can?
On that terrible day when we lost fifty thousand of our men.
On that day when it looked like all was lost.
Only now do I look back and see that I was alive.
Only now do I realise how much I loved that day.

It was the time of my life

A time where my life hung by a thread

I was living…I was breathing. My army and I were making
history.

* *

I can feel my heart pounding, I can feel the air of anticipation
that battle brings, my hands are sweaty and my head feels
light, this is the time where battles are won or lost, I must
have clarity.

* *

On the battlefield life and death is such a narrow margin,

An archer who runs out of arrows,

A sword that breaks,

If I turn left instead of right,

If I blink at the wrong time,

If I thrust instead of parry,

Your life can end in a single moment for indecision.

When all around is screaming and men falling

You must somehow stay composed.

Somehow know everything around you,

If I step in a hole and fall…I may give my enemy the time
to strike,

Just moments! Just moments are between life and death!

* *

I can feel my heart pounding,

The sweat on my brow begins

In the distance, I see men…our men,

They shake the land as we go forward,

There is a shiver down my spine

I clench my sword tightly,

Soon it begins…soon we attack!

By nightfall we would have won the field…today we fight like heroes,

Today we grind our opponents into the dirt!

* *

Is there any stronger feeling than vengeance?

As with most feelings, does it wane over the passage of time?

Does it destroy the person who wishes it?

Does it rot away inside him, till he thinks of nothing else?

When vengeance is mixed with slavery and imprisonment, what concoction will that produce?

It produces a man who cares nothing of his own life, a man who feels nothing other than the obsession for freedom.

How do we control such intense despair? How do we stop ourselves from becoming like those we fight?

Is there a price for freedom that is too great?

Is there a line we cross over because we feel we are just?

It is the measure of the men we are, and it will be the measure by which we are judged by our future generations.

Will our cause be called just? Or will our vengeance be called rabid lust?

We must battle our own pasts and confront our own demons before we embark on our vengeance.

We must know what is right and believe which is wrong.

We must show everyone that we are men, men who have been wronged, but men who fight with honour and forbearance.

By our sacrifices, we make a nation, with our pain we forge a future, with our justice we put our children on the right path of becoming men.

What we do now decides their fate; do we want our children

to be slaves of tyranny? Or do we give them the platform of greatness.

Gentleman the future is ours, how our children live in it might be the most important battle we ever face.

**

It is our children who we truly love...everything else comes a very distant second.

**

Where has, the child gone?

Where has the boy, who looked at the world with such optimism and wonder disappeared to? Will he ever return?

**

Bad luck and broken

Where has all the fun gone from life?

Why is now only trouble and strife?

When will it end? How much longer can it be?

Endless tunnel of dark is now all I see

Bad news and woe is constant now it seems

Reality of life is now shattered dreams

Struggle every day, trying to survive

Fuck this bollocks, there must be more to life

**

Say nothing! Do nothing, Walk quietly,

Make patience your friend

Forget haste

Only a man without thought rushes in

**

So, it ends
So, our battle is over
What cometh of me now my liege
What cometh of these hands
The hands which held my sword for you
What cometh of the pride in my heart
The pride that I follow the greatest man I have ever known
Where do I go now?
What shall I do now without your commands
My worth is beside you my liege
Maybe I should perish in this last battle
For without the sound of your voice on the battlefield
Filling my soul with passion, pride, I have no place
I am your commander of war
What shall I do now. Sow crops

Quotes about inspiration

If you continue when your body is screaming at you in pain
Then that pain will turn to satisfaction
If you quit, then that pain will stay with you for a lifetime

* *.

You will keep on moving forward
You will give it everything you have
You will feel the joy of succeeding
You will become a man you want to see
You will be proud of your life
You will live life free of doubts

You will win! You will move forward
You will never go back, never give in to failure
Through winning, you become one with your soul
If you accept failure, you refuse to live.

* *

When people can't do something
They like to tell you they you can't do it!
I love it when someone says it can't be done

* *

It is better to die once on your feet
Than die every day on your knees

Quotes about Fear

They asked me if in my heart, I feel fear from thy enemy, I
replied that all they can do is hurt my body but my heart can
only be hurt by those whom I love

* *

What is fear, can I taste it, can I feel it, can I hold it, if I cannot
do these simple things then how can I control it

* *

When the battle is here, whom shall be more fearful, the
enemy or I who have nothing left to lose

* *

Is there anything you fear?
Only fear itself

* *

My brother, why do you not show fear?
Brave ... I know you are but are you foolish not to show the
emotions that plague other men

* *

Once this wrath within me is unleashed you will suffer fear like
only the gods can create
If I fear for one moment then my hand my shake, if I fear for
moment then my judgement may be biased, I cannot fear,
I must be strong for my people for if they see weakness in me
then this war is lost.

* *

What a toll this life takes from me, what of my soul, what toll
will my children have to bear for my actions, doubt, I hate it,
I detest it, what games my nature plays with me, I kill like no
other man has killed before, then my soul rips me apart.

* *

I must do what I do not want to do, I have lived through these
horrors and I am still here, I have touched the face of evil and
tailored it for my own means, what shall I fear, what can fear
do to me, I am the total embodiment of what I fear the most

* *

You are fearless, you are the warrior, the face of salvation to
your people and the face of terror and doom to your enemy

* *

To be a leader of men, I cannot be a follower of fear

* *

Fear causes more damage before a battle than any sword
during it

* *

Is it true they call me death?
Is my life a curse with every breath?
Do I feel sorrow, do I feel shame?
What of my soul in this endless epic game?
Will I be respected or will I be feared?
Cursed, tainted …commonly cheered
Will I be remembered as a man or a king?
A hero or a horror. Just a bloodthirsty thing

* *

Why can I not cry?
What stops me from pain?
Why does death not affect me anymore/
What am I becoming?
I want my feelings back!
I want to know what it feels like to show remorse,
I want to know what it feels like to be a man again,
I am hollow now,
I look at myself in the mirror and I see a stranger
I see empty eyes
I see coldness
I see nothing
God help me…save me from myself.
It was a time of angst
It was a time of woe
Where it would end
We just didn't know
We fought like warriors, refused to retreat
Refused to accept we could ever be beat
Battle after battle we left men in the dirt

Eyes of vengeance, hearts of hurt
It never mattered to us where we pointed the gun
Nothing else mattered more that we won
But in all this glory, victory and death
We destroyed men like matchsticks till nothing was left
Taking no prisoners, no chains on their feet
We forgot we have souls and a maker to meet.

* *

A still tongue keeps a wise head

* *

Don't dabble with the devil unless you are prepared for him to
dabble with you.

* *

Play with bees then someday you will get stung.

* *

A man cannot always be judged by the ways in which those
beneath him act.

Joe Pyle Jnr in the Monday club (Peckham)
Credit: Jocelyn Bain Hogg

Ending or the beginning?

JOE Pyle Jnr is now one of the most successful professional boxing managers in the UK. He spends his time taking care of his family and his boxers – what's next for him? Like Joe says "You never know just what is around the corner, one day you can be bored stiff and the next day you cannot think straight from work. I keep my options open and live as I have always lived … day by day! It makes me laugh when people around me hear their phone ring and don't answer and then they say they cannot be bothered! I just laugh and shake my head as they haven't got my mantra… 'answer the call! You never know it could be a call which changes your life!"

Trevor Cattouse – Roy Shaw – Joe Pyle Jnr – Deano

Joe Pyle Jnr & Snr & Ray Winstone

Joe Pyle Jnr & Mitch Pyle
Photo credit: Jocelyn Bain Hogg

Joe Pyle Jnr – Tony Lambrianou – Terry Inns

Joe Pyle Snr – Jimmy White – Alan P – Joe Pyle Jnr – Patsy Palmer

Roy Shaw & Joe Pyle Jnr

Joe Pyle Snr & Jnr

Be safe and remember there are
Seven deadly sins....
pride, greed, lust, envy, gluttony, wrath, and sloth

JP Jnr